Glowing fitness,

The successful way to lower cholesterol

inner health

Low cholesterol – low fat

The latest research tells us that everyday cholesterol consciousness means eating a low-fat diet in order to keep the cholesterol down. A change in cooking habits is the route to success. The delicious recipes in this book make that change easy. You will soon recognize the benefits, even if you are only watching the cholesterol on behalf of someone else. What is good for your arteries is also great for your figure.

Knowing your level of risk

Babies have a blood cholesterol level between 60-120mg per 100ml. In adults, it ought not to exceed 200mg per 100ml, but many people have cholesterol levels above this critical limit. The problem is that the gradual loss of elasticity and narrowing of the arteries can go unnoticed. These changes can make a person twenty years older inside than they appear outwardly. The fact is, arteriosclerosis can develop without showing symptoms until a heart attack occurs. A medical check-up is the only sure way to achieve certainty.

MORE THAN ONE TYPE OF CHOLESTEROL

* Dietary cholesterol is only found in foods of animal origin. Your food should not contain more than 300mg of this type of cholesterol a day (the equivalent of eating one egg). People with high cholesterol levels should have no more than 250mg.

* Blood cholesterol does to some extent come from what we eat, but 80 per cent of it is made by the body itself. The body's cholesterol production goes down if we eat too much cholesterol in our diet. However, there is more than one type of cholesterol. It is dangerous to have a high level of LDL (Low-Density Lipoprotein) cholesterol. It transports cholesterol to all the cells of the body, and levels over 140mg per 100ml of blood are unhealthy. However, a high level of HDL (High-Density Lipoprotein) cholesterol is good. It takes excess cholesterol to be broken down in the liver.

KEY TIPS FOR HEALTH

* Eat a low-fat diet. Choose the sort of fats that contain mono-unsaturated and polyunsaturated fatty acids in preference to the ones with saturated fatty acids.

* Avoid excessive cholesterol intake. For most people, there is no benefit in eating a diet that is extremely low in cholesterol. The body usually produces the amount of cholesterol it needs.

* Select foods that are high in fibre.

* Practise sports that build stamina, like running and swimming, and reduce stress.

FOODS HIGH IN CHOLESTEROL OR SATURATED FATTY ACIDS

FOOD ITEM PER 100 g	CHOL mg	FAT g	SAT. FAT g	P/S-QUO-TIENT*
MILK, DAIRY PRODUCTS, EGGS				
milk, 3.5 % fat	11	3.5	2.1	0.05
cream, 30 % fat	109	31.7	18.2	0.05
cream cheese 47 % fat	84	28	18.9	0.05
Camembert 24 % fat	93	33.2	20.3	0.05
edam 25 % fat	59	28.3	17.5	0.04
Emmenthal 25 % fat	70	30	17.9	0.06
1 egg yolk (19 g)	314	6.1	1.7	0.6

FATS, OILS				
butter	240	83.2	48.1	0.06
rendered butter	340	99.5	60.8	0.08
lard	86	99.7	38.5	0.3
coconut oil	1	99	86.6	0.01

FISH, SEAFOOD				
herring	77	17.8	3.3	0.6
eel	164	24.5	5.7	0.4
oysters	260	1.2	0.5	0.2

MEAT, POULTRY, SAUSAGE AND MEAT PRODUCTS				
duck	70	17.2	4.8	0.6
goose	75	31	8.9	0.5
beef (leg)	120	7.1	3.7	0.05
pork (leg)	86	22.9	9.6	0.4
liver (pig)	346	4.5	1.6	0.7
minced pork	70	27.5	9.7	0.1
liver sausage(coarse)	85	29.2	11.4	0.1
ham (boiled)	85	19.5	1.3	0.3

*See page 4: How much fat and which kind?

The low-cholesterol
low-fat eating made for enjoyment
way to health

THE RECIPE FOR SUCCESS: KEEP DOWN THE FAT

* Limit your daily intake of fat to 55-75g. That is equivalent to the recommended proportion of fat in the diet: given an energy requirement of 2000kcal per day for women and 2400kcal for men, fat then accounts for 25-30 percent of daily energy intake. You can speed up your success and lose weight by eating just 1500kcal per day, of which 40-50g is fat.

* Watch for hidden fat when shopping. High-fat foods are usually high in cholesterol too (table, page 3).

GOOD FAT AND OTHER KINDS

* Fats that contain saturated fatty acids drive up your cholesterol level. They are the main type in animal produce such as meat, cheese, lard, and butter, but coconut oil and palm kernel oil also consist mainly of saturated fat, despite their vegetable origin.

* Trans fatty acids increase cholesterol levels. These are found in the oils used for frying, in spray-on fats used in the baking trade, and processed foods that contain hydrogenated fats, especially cakes, biscuits, and ready-made meals.

* Fats and oils that contain mono-unsaturated fatty acids reduce cholesterol levels. Olive oil is rich in these.

* Fats and oils that contain polyunsaturated fatty acids (especially linoleic acid) bring down cholesterol levels. Sunflower oil is a source of these.

HOW MUCH FAT AND WHICH KIND?

* The ideal balance is for no more than one third of fat intake to come from saturated fats, and no more than one third from polyunsaturated fats. At least one third should be mono-unsaturated.

* There should be more polyunsaturates than saturates in a healthy diet. If you divide the proportion of polyunsaturates by the saturates, that is the P/S quotient. So keep your P/S quotient (table, page 3; also see next point) above 1.

WHICH FAT TO USE WHEN

* For salads, use cold-pressed oils. They reduce cholesterol levels. Sunflower oil (15.8), walnut oil (14.2), and safflower oil (8.3) have a high P/S quotient. Rapeseed oil has a good combination of unsaturated fatty acids.

* For cooking, cold-pressed olive oil is ideal. It is high in mono-unsaturated fatty acids.
* Butter contains cholesterol, but very few unhealthy fatty acids.
* Oily fish such as herring and salmon contain beneficial omega-3 fatty acids, which do not raise cholesterol levels. Other sources are rapeseed (canola) oil, walnut oil, and soya oil.

LOW-FAT COOKING TIPS

* STIR-FRY food in a small amount of oil, turning constantly, in a wok or deep frying pan. Keep the cooking time short.
* DRY-FRY in a hot frying pan with the minimum of oil. The key is to brown or cook the food until translucent over a low heat, lifting and loosening it repeatedly with a spatula.
* STOVE-TOP GRILLING browns the food on a griddle lightly brushed with oil.
* STEAMING is a gentle cooking method and extremely low fat. All you need is an expandable steamer and a saucepan with a well-fitting lid.
* COOK FOOD IN ITS OWN JUICES This gentle method saves on fat and preserves vitamin content. The lower the heat, the better the results.
* PAPILLOTES are individually wrapped in parchment. The food inside, such as fish or vegetables, is steamed, keeping fat and cholesterol low.
* USE A TEASPOON to measure out the oil, and choose a fragrant, cold-pressed oil. Heat it gently and do not let it become smoking hot. The only oil that can bear higher temperatures (up to 200°C/400°F) is olive oil.
* BIND SAUCES with unroasted carob bean flour. It has no cholesterol. Replace cream with cultured milk, yoghurt, buttermilk, or reduced-fat soured cream.
* SEA SALT is easy to measure out. That is important for anyone with high blood pressure.

Healthy-

Everyday health food

option foods

CHOOSING WISELY

❋ All fresh fruit and vegetables are cholesterol-free. They contain secondary plant substances that keep arteries elastic. Look particularly for fruit and vegetables that are rich in anti-oxidants like vitamin C and carotenoids (found in yellow and dark green vegetables). They protect against oxidation - oxidized LDL cholesterol tends to collect on the walls of blood vessels.

❋ High-fibre foods: whole-grain produce, vegetables, fruit, and potatoes. Fibre can reduce cholesterol levels.

❋ Choose low-cholesterol and low-fat options when buying milk, dairy produce, meat, poultry, sausages, and meat products.

❋ Fish that is low in fat and cholesterol is good for your health – but so is oily fish (mackerel, herring, salmon) that contains omega-3 fatty acids. These do not raise blood cholesterol.

❋ Eat just small portions of fats, oils, nuts and seeds rich in unsaturates, linoleic acid, and vitamin E. They can lower blood cholesterol.

❋ Use spices and other flavourings with a positive effect on health.

The table opposite lists suitable foods to choose if you want to lower your blood cholesterol and fat levels.

COOK CLEVER

You will obtain best results if you keep your fat consumption low and design your meals to keep the proportion of fat between 25 and 30 per cent. The seven-day Powerfood plan (pages 8-9) gives examples. Avoid foods that are high in cholesterol (table, page 3). Use less fat in cooking, and use more vegetable stock, either in addition or as a complete substitute for fat.

Choose products that are proven to lower cholesterol levels. If you drink tea, try green tea. It has a beneficial effect on blood cholesterol. Look for organically grown tea. If you are a coffee drinker, choose filter coffee. It has a neutral effect on cholesterol levels.

SUITABLE FOODS FOR LOWERING BLOOD CHOLESTEROL AND FAT LEVELS

FISH, POULTRY, MEAT
- chicken breast
- cod
- herring
- mackerel
- pike/perch
- pollock
- quail
- rabbit
- salmon
- skipjack tuna
- trout
- tuna
- turkey breast

FRUIT
- all fresh fruit
- apples
- bananas
- bilberries
- blackberries
- blackcurrants
- blueberries
- cranberries
- dried fruit
- figs
- gooseberries
- grapes
- green olives
- greengages
- kiwi fruit
- mandarins
- nectarines
- papayas
- pears
- pineapples
- quinces
- raspberries
- redcurrants
- rhubarb
- strawberries

GRAIN ETC.
- barley
- brown rice
- buckwheat
- bulghur wheat
- couscous
- millet
- oats
- polenta
- rye
- spelt
- wheat
- wholewheat
- pasta

MILK, DAIRY PRODUCE, EGGS
- buttermilk
- cheese, less than 30% fat
- cottage cheese
- cultured milk
- egg white
- kefir
- milk, skimmed
- low-fat
- quark, 0.2%
- yoghurt, low-fat

NUTS, SEEDS
- almonds
- hazelnuts
- peanuts
- pumpkin seeds
- sesame seeds
- sunflower seeds
- walnuts

PULSES
- beans
- chickpeas
- lentils
- peas
- soya beans

SPICES
- capers
- cardamom
- chervil
- chilli
- fenugreek
- garlic
- ginger
- horseradish
- mustardseed
- rosemary
- saffron
- soy sauce
- tarragon
- turmeric

VEGETABLES
- all fresh vegetables
- artichokes
- aubergines (eggplant)
- bean sprouts etc.
- beetroot
- bell peppers
- broccoli
- Brussels sprouts
- carrots
- celeriac
- chard
- Chinese cabbage
- cress
- dandelion
- endive
- fennel
- green beans
- green cabbage
- Jerusalem artichoke
- lamb's lettuce
- leek
- nettle
- onion
- parsnip
- peas
- potatoes
- rocket
- scorzonera
- shiitake mushrooms
- sorrel
- spinach
- sweet potatoes
- sweetcorn
- turnip
- white cabbage

Seven-day

a treat for body and soul

Powerfood plan

WELLNESS IN A WEEK

Do you want to bring down your cholesterol level and shed a few pounds? Treat yourself to a week of healthier eating and improving your fitness. The best way to bring your cholesterol under control is to eat a mainly vegetarian diet. Enjoy luscious health food. Stave off hunger in between meals with your favourite fruit and vegetables. Buy organic produce, and go to the best greengrocery supplier in town, even if it costs a little more. Seek out good quality. Tea or green tea makes the ideal drink. It has a calming effect and helps you lower your cholesterol levels.

REDUCE STRESS

Reduce your stress as much as you can: this lowers your cholesterol level. Make space to unwind. Research into human happiness lists cooking among the creative pursuits. It can bring great contentment, as long as the stress stays out of the kitchen. Take some exercise every day to complement your dietary plan and ensure lasting results. Choose a sport you enjoy, of the sort that builds stamina, such as running, swimming, inline skating, or another sport that

appeals. To burn off fat, the recipe for success is at least 30 minutes' activity, every day if possible, and preferably in the morning. In any case, you should exercise at least three times a week.

THE SEVEN-DAY PLAN

The plan gives suggestions for breakfast and main meals for each day. You can vary the plan to suit you, but make sure you include plenty of fresh fruit and vegetables. You should eat them at the beginning of the meal for the greatest benefit. Unless you have a weight problem, you can add a vegetable accompaniment to any of the main dishes, as long as you do not increase fat intake.

You will find some main course dishes for one-pot preparation. Some are suitable for freezing, so those pressed for time can make enough for several meals at once. The chapter on salads and finger food contains recipes that are very quick to prepare and suitable to take to work.

PLAN FOR THE WEEK

Monday

* Breakfast of yoghurt and an apple; one rye bread roll with fruit spread
* Fresh melon wedges * Soya noodles with vegetables
* Tomatoes with cress * Bean soup with tofu * Gooseberry and almond snow

Tuesday

* Breakfast of orange and carrot juice; multi-grain baguette with tomato and cheese
* Brussels sprout and walnut confit * Gremolata risotto
* A few radishes * Light cream of carrot soup * Bulghur wheat with melon

Wednesday

* Breakfast of muesli with milk and fruit; wholewheat roll
* Orange halves * Bean curry with tandoori
* Dandelion with fennel * Purslane with chicken

Thursday

* Breakfast of yoghurt-quark with herbs, carrots, peppers and rustic bread
* Fresh pineapple rings * Baked cannelloni
* Lamb's lettuce with bean sprouts * Mixed berry dessert with rice

Friday

* Breakfast of muesli with kefir, apple, and banana
* Pink grapefruit halves * Cod with vegetables
* Apple and potato salad * Vanilla pears with quark cream quenelles

Saturday

* Breakfast of orange juice, a rye baguette with roast turkey and cucumber
* Rocket salad with bulghur wheat * Sicilian caponatina
* Spring onions with miso dip * Grilled green asparagus * Kefir with raspberries

Sunday

* Sweet kasha with citrus salad
* Fresh figs * Penne with tomatoes
* Pumpkin and cranberry salad * Quail en papillote * Quinces with cinnamon yoghurt

Dandelion

with papaya

fruit vinaigrette

fennel

Serves 2: • 100g (3¹/₂ oz) dandelion leaves • 1 fennel bulb • 1 papaya • ¹/₂ bunch coriander (cilantro) leaves • ¹/₂ tsp olive oil • 1 tbsp cider vinegar • 3 tbsp vegetable stock • sea salt • pepper

Wash and trim the dandelion leaves and fennel. Peel and pit the papaya and dice one half. Wash the coriander, shake dry, and puree it with the remaining papaya, 1 teaspoon of oil, the vinegar, and the stock. Season the vinaigrette with salt and pepper. Heat a griddle, and brush with the remaining oil. Slice the fennel bulb and stalk, season with salt and pepper, and grill for 4 minutes on each side. Arrange the fennel with the dandelion leaves, vinaigrette, and diced papaya to serve.

PER PORTION: 103 kcal • 4 g protein • 3 g fat • 15 g carbohydrate • 0 mg cholesterol

Lamb's lettuce

with freshly grated horseradish

with bean sprouts

Serves 2: • 50g (scant 2oz) lamb's lettuce • 50g (scant 2oz) bean sprouts • 250g (9oz) beetroot • sea salt • pepper • 10g (¹/₃ oz) freshly grated horseradish • 1 tbsp cider vinegar • 4 tbsp vegetable stock • ¹/₂ tsp walnut oil

Wash and trim the lamb's lettuce, and wash the bean sprouts. Peel and grate the beetroot, and season with salt and pepper. Stir together the horseradish, cider vinegar, vegetable stock, oil, salt, and pepper. Mix the bean sprouts into the vinaigrette. Arrange the lamb's lettuce and beetroot on plates and sprinkle with the vinaigrette mixture.

PER PORTION: 55 kcal • 3 g protein • 2 g fat • 8 g carbohydrate • 0 mg cholesterol

Pumpkin and

with rapeseed oil and piquant chilli

cranberry salad

Serves 2: • 250 g (9oz) pumpkin • ¹/₄ frisee lettuce • 1 red chilli • 1 tbsp honey • 50g (scant 2oz) cranberries • ¹/₂ tsp rapeseed (canola) oil • 1 tbsp cider vinegar • 4 tbsp vegetable stock • sea salt • pepper

Peel and grate the pumpkin. Wash, trim, and separate the lettuce. Slit open the chilli, remove the seeds, wash it, and dice very finely. Heat the honey and diced chilli in a saucepan. Add the cranberries, and caramelize until the liquid thickens. Add the oil, vinegar, and stock, bring to the boil, and season with salt and pepper. Serve the lettuce and pumpkin in the dressing.

PER PORTION: 55 kcal • 1 g protein • 2 g fat • 9 g carbohydrate • 0 mg cholesterol

Rocket salad with

with scorzonera crisps

bulghur wheat

Preheat the oven to 150°C (300°F). Line a baking sheet with parchment. Bring the stock to the boil in a small saucepan. Stir in the bulghur wheat, return to boiling point, and cook for 5 minutes on a low heat, stirring. Set aside for 15 minutes for the wheat to swell.

Wash the scorzonera, peel it (ideally wear kitchen gloves), and grate into very thin slices. Season immediately with salt and powdered hot paprika. Spread the slices on the baking tray, and dry in the middle of the oven for 10 minutes.

For the dressing, mix the coriander, yoghurt, cumin, and orange juice. Season well with salt and pepper. Trim, sort, and wash the rocket. Shake dry. Tear into bite-sized pieces if necessary. Arrange on plates, top with bulghur wheat, and sprinkle with dressing. Serve the scorzonera crisps separately.

Serves 2:

baking parchment

4-5 tbsp vegetable stock

20g ($^3/_4$ oz) bulghur wheat

2 scorzonera

sea salt

1 pinch of hot red paprika

1 tbsp chopped coriander (cilantro) leaves

4 tbsp low-fat yoghurt

$^1/_2$ tsp cumin

2 tbsp orange juice

pepper

50g (scant 2oz) rocket (arugula)

Rocket

This popular salad herb is also called rucola (arugula). It is related to cabbage and mustard. Its flavour and its beneficial effect on blood cholesterol levels are derived from the mustard oils it contains.

PER PORTION:

83 kcal

4 g protein

1 g fat

15 g carbohydrate

0 mg cholesterol

Apple and
with fresh rosemary
potato salad

Preheat the oven to 180°C (350°F). Wash the potatoes, slice in half without peeling, and place on a baking sheet cut side uppermost. Sprinkle with salt, pepper, and

Serves 2:

2 firm cooking potatoes (80g/3oz each)

sea salt

black pepper

½ tsp rosemary leaves

1 tbsp cider vinegar

4 tbsp vegetable stock

1 tsp sunflower oil

1 apple

1 small red onion

½ lollo rosso lettuce

rosemary, and bake in the middle of the oven for about 20 minutes.

Stir together the vinegar, stock, oil, salt, and pepper to make the vinaigrette. Set aside 2 teaspoons of vinaigrette. Wash the apple in hot water, dry, and core it. It may be used unpeeled if wished. Cut into small dice, and mix into the vinaigrette. Peel the onion, dice finely, and add. Wash the lettuce, spin it dry, and separate it into pieces.

Hollow out the potatoes, leaving the skins intact. Set aside. Dice the flesh finely and mix into the vinaigrette. Fill the potato skins with the mixture. Turn the lollo rosso in the remaining vinaigrette, arrange on plates, and place the potato halves on top.

An apple a day

Studies show that eating several raw apples a day can lower blood cholesterol and raise the level of protective HDL cholesterol. This effect is due to the pectin in the apples. It is also the pectin that satisfies.

PER PORTION:

103 kcal

2 g protein

2 g fat

19 g carbohydrate

0 mg cholesterol

Brussels sprout
finger food with chicory leaves
and walnut confit

Serves 2:

150g (5oz) Brussels sprouts
1 red onion
1 tbsp honey
1 tbsp chopped walnuts
1 tbsp cider vinegar
4 tbsp vegetable stock
sea salt
black pepper
2 heads of chicory

Wash and trim the sprouts. Cut into quarters. Peel the onion and dice finely. Caramelize the honey in a small saucepan over a medium heat, until thickened but still liquid. Immediately stir in the sprouts, diced onion, and walnuts. Add the cider vinegar and vegetable stock. Boil over a low heat until the quantity is reduced to 2 tablespoons. Season with salt and pepper. Spoon the confit into stemmed dessert dishes or champagne glasses and cool before serving.

Meanwhile separate the leaves of the chicory, wash and drain. Insert the leaves decoratively into the confit by their ends, to spoon it out as a dip. Place each glass on a plate with a napkin to serve.

Walnuts

Although walnuts have a high oil content, it is a nutritionally valuable oil. They consist mainly of mono-unsaturates and polyunsaturates, and have a high P/S quotient (see pages 4-5) of 8.5. Walnuts therefore reduce your cholesterol level. Nevertheless, you should limit your intake to 15g ($^1/_2$ oz) per day.

PER PORTION:

105 kcal

5 g protein

4 g fat

12 g carbohydrate

0 mg cholesterol

power

Spring onions
elegant, low-fat finger food
with miso dip

Trim the spring onions, leaving as much green as possible. Wash and cut them into pieces roughly 5cm (2in) long. Remove the stalk, seeds, and ribs from the yellow peppers and wash them. Cut into lengthwise strips about 1cm (1/2 in) in width. Place a griddle on a medium heat to become hot. Spear alternate pieces of spring onion and yellow pepper on the skewers. Season with salt and pepper. Brush the griddle with the olive oil. Grill the vegetable skewers for about 4 minutes each side over a low heat.

Meanwhile make the dip. Peel and crush the garlic. Mix the miso and tamari, and stir in the sesame oil, coriander, and ginger. Season the dip with salt and pepper, and transfer to small bowls.

Arrange the skewers on a serving plate, and serve with the bowls of miso dip. Cherry tomatoes on a bed of cress, julienne of cucumber and carrot, and thin strips of flat bread browned on the griddle are all suitable accompaniments.

Serves 2:

250g (9oz) spring onions
1 1/2 yellow peppers
4 wooden skewers
sea salt
black pepper
1/2 tsp olive oil
1 clove of garlic
40g (1 1/2 oz) miso (Oriental store)
1 tsp tamari (Japanese soy sauce)
1/2 tsp sesame oil
1 tsp coriander (cilantro) leaves
1 tsp freshly grated ginger

PER PORTION: 105 kcal • 6 g protein • 5 g fat • 13 g carbohydrate • 0 mg cholesterol

Soya noodles

stir fried with minimum fat

with vegetables

Bring a generous quantity of salted water to the boil in a saucepan. Break the spaghetti into shorter noodles and cook until firm to the bite, according to packet instructions. Meanwhile, peel and chop the onions. Wash, peel, and grate the carrots and celeriac. Peel and grate the ginger and garlic. Drain the noodles.

Place a wok or large, deep frying pan on a medium heat to become hot. Add and heat the oil. Turn the ginger and garlic in the oil, then add the onion, carrot, and celeriac. Stir fry for about 3 minutes. Pour on the vegetable stock and bring to the boil. Add the drained noodles and stir fry for about 1 minute. Season with salt, pepper, and soy sauce.

Serves 2:
sea salt
160g (5 ¹/₂oz) soya noodles (spaghetti)
1 large red onion
4 carrots
100g (3 ¹/₂oz) celeriac
30g (1oz) fresh ginger (1 piece about 7cm/2 ³/₄in long)
1 clove of garlic
1 tsp olive oil
100ml (3 ¹/₂fl oz) vegetable stock
black pepper
1 tsp soy sauce

PER PORTION:
382 Kcal
13 g protein
3 g fat
74 g carbohydrate
0 mg cholesterol

Pasta – the ideal accompaniment
The fibre content of wholewheat pasta makes it perfect for the cholesterol-conscious. It contains three times the fibre of traditional pasta. Durum wheat pasta without egg is cholesterol-free.

Spaghetti with

al dente with sweet and sour seasoning

curried aubergine

Serves 2: • 160 g (5 ½ oz) wholewheat spaghetti • sea salt • 2 onions • 3 tomatoes • 1 aubergine (eggplant) • 1 tsp olive oil • 4 tsp currants • 1 tbsp curry powder • pepper • 1 tsp honey • 1 tbsp vinegar • 100ml (3 ½ fl oz) vegetable stock

Following packet instructions, cook the spaghetti in plenty of boiling salted water until al dente. Peel and chop the onions. Remove the tough stalk parts from the tomatoes and aubergine. Dice. Heat the oil. Turn the onions, tomatoes, aubergine, and currants in this for 5 minutes. Season with salt, curry powder, pepper, honey, and vinegar. Add the stock; boil. Drain and serve the pasta; top with sauce.

PER PORTION: 398 kcal • 16 g protein • 5 g fat • 72 g carbohydrate • 0 mg cholesterol

Penne

pumpkin seeds add flair

with tomatoes

Serves 2: • 160 g (5 ½ oz) durum wheat penne • sea salt • 3 tomatoes • 6 spring onions

• 2 tbsp pumpkin seeds • 2 tbsp balsamic vinegar • 1 tsp pumpkin seed oil

• 140 ml (scant 5fl oz) vegetable stock • pepper

Cook the penne according to instructions until al dente. Wash the tomatoes, remove the tough stem area, and cut into eighths. Wash and trim the spring onions. Chop, including the green parts. Toast the pumpkin seeds briefly in a pan without fat. Stir in the spring onions and tomatoes; fry for 1 minute. Add the vinegar, oil, and stock; boil. Season with salt and pepper, and turn the pasta in the mixture.

PER PORTION: 413 kcal • 16 g protein • 10 g fat • 68 g carbohydrate • 0 mg cholesterol

Baked
with chard and olive filling
cannelloni

Preheat the oven to 180°C (350°F). Pre-cook the cannelloni according to instructions in plenty of salted water. Refresh with cold water; drain. Peel the garlic. Wash the tomatoes, remove the tough stem parts, and dice. Place the diced tomato in a small saucepan. Crush and add the garlic. Add the stock, bring to the boil, and add half the thyme, the nutmeg, salt, and pepper. Cover and cook for 5 minutes. Wash and drain the chard. Separate the stems and the leaves, and cut both into strips. Peel and chop the onions. Pit and chop the olives.

Add the oil to a frying pan over a medium heat. When hot, fry the onions, chard stems, and olives for 3 minutes. Add the chard leaves and continue cooking for 1 minute. Season with salt, pepper, and the remaining thyme. Fill the cannelloni with this mixture. Coat the bottom of an ovenproof dish with half the tomato sauce. Place the cannelloni on this, and cover with the remaining tomato sauce. Mix the breadcrumbs, parsley, and Parmesan, and sprinkle on top. Bake in the middle of the oven for 20-30 minutes.

Serves 2:

8 durum wheat cannelloni

sea salt

1 clove of garlic

2 tomatoes

100ml (3 ½ fl oz) vegetable stock

2 tsp thyme

1 pinch of nutmeg

black pepper

500g (18oz) chard

2 red onions

6 green olives

1 tsp olive oil

40g (1 ½ oz) wholewheat breadcrumbs

2 tbsp chopped parsley

20g (³/₄ oz) freshly grated Parmesan

Per Portion: 455 kcal • 22 g protein • 8 g fat • 72 g carbohydrate • 6 mg cholesterol

with a kefir and turmeric sauce

Serves 2:
2 red onions
120g (4oz) fresh shiitake mushrooms
1 tsp olive oil
160g (5 ¹/₂oz) brown short-grain rice
400ml (14fl oz) vegetable stock
sea salt
black pepper
1 tsp turmeric
100ml (3 ¹/₂ fl oz) kefir (or probiotic yoghurt drink)
1 tbsp chopped flat-leaf parsley

Peel and chop the onions. Wipe the mushrooms with a damp cloth, remove the stems, and slice the caps thinly. Heat the oil in a saucepan over a medium heat. Add the rice, onions, and mushrooms, and cook, stirring, for about 3 minutes until translucent. Add 360ml (12fl oz) of the stock and bring to the boil. Cover and cook over a low heat for 30-40 minutes. Then season with salt and pepper. About 5 minutes before the rice is cooked, bring the remaining stock to the boil with the turmeric and set aside. Whisk in the kefir with a hand blender. Heat the sauce, but do not boil. Season with salt and pepper. Mix in the parsley. Serve the kefir and turmeric sauce with the pilaf

Shiitake mushrooms – flavour and refinement

These mushrooms from Japan have a cholesterol-lowering effect – fresh ones more than dried. They are now being grown successfully in Europe, and are available all year round in well-run greengrocery stores. They can be used in the same way as button mushrooms, but lose hardly any liquid during cooking.

PER PORTION:

546 kcal

14 g protein

7 g fat

112 g carbohydrate

4 mg cholesterol

Gremolata
with brown rice and fresh mushrooms
risotto

Peel and chop the onions and garlic. Wash and trim the mushrooms, and cut into small dice. Heat the oil in a saucepan over a medium heat, and cook the onions and garlic until translucent. Add the mushrooms and rice, and cook gently for about 3 minutes, stirring. Pour on the vegetable stock and bring to the boil. Cover and cook over a low heat for about 30 minutes. Continue cooking if necessary to evaporate any remaining cooking liquid.

Make the gremolata by mixing the parsley with 2 teaspoons of lemon zest and 1 teaspoon of orange zest. Season the risotto with salt and pepper, and sprinkle with gremolata. Serve with a mixed salad.

Serves 2:
2 red onions
1 clove of garlic
**200g (7oz) button mushrooms
or boletus**
½ tsp olive oil
**160g (5 ½oz) brown short-grain
rice**
**360ml (12fl oz) unsalted vegetable
stock**
1 tbsp chopped flat-leaf parsley
zest of 1 unwaxed lemon
zest of 1 unwaxed orange
sea salt, black pepper

Brown rice

Unpolished brown rice is an important source of fibre. Its fibre content is three times that of polished, white rice. The portion of brown rice in this recipe provides one tenth of the daily requirement.

PER PORTION:

348 kcal

9 g protein

5 g fat

66 g carbohydrate

1 mg cholesterol

power

Fragrant rice with
with aromatic coriander purée
sugar snap peas

Cover the rice with water and soak for 30 minutes. Drain. Bring to the boil in 200ml (7fl oz) fresh water. Add salt, cover, and cook over a low heat for 20 minutes.

Meanwhile wash the coriander leaves or parsley, shake dry, remove the tough stalks, and chop. Add the rapeseed oil, 1 tablespoon of stock, salt, and pepper, and purée with a hand blender.

Wash and trim the sugar snap peas, and cut diagonally into pieces about 2cm (3/4 in) long. Peel and chop the onions. Heat the olive oil in a frying pan over a medium heat, and fry the onions and carrots for about 4 minutes, until translucent. Add the sugar snap peas, and continue to cook for another 2 minutes, stirring. Pour on the remaining stock and bring to the boil. Season with salt, pepper, and tamari. Serve the rice separately or mixed with the vegetables, as wished. The coriander purée should be served separately.

Serves 2:

160g (5 1/2 oz) brown basmati rice

sea salt

1 bunch of coriander (cilantro) leaves or flat-leaf parsley

1 tsp rapeseed oil

110ml (3 3/4 fl oz) vegetable stock

black pepper

200g (7oz) sugar snap peas

4 carrots

2 red onions

1 tsp olive oil

4 tbsp tamari (Japanese soy sauce)

PER PORTION: 474 kcal • 35 g protein • 10 g fat • 122 g carbohydrate • 0 mg cholesterol

Grilled green asparagus

with tasty roasted polenta

Peel and chop the onions. Bring the vegetable stock to the boil in a saucepan, add salt, and slowly stir in the polenta with a balloon whisk. Allow to swell, stirring frequently, for about 8 minutes. Stir the parsley and nutmeg into the polenta. Transfer the polenta to a large plate, smooth it down with a palette knife, and cool. Preheat the oven to 70°C (160°F).

Meanwhile, wash the asparagus and peel the lower third. Cut the stems in half across and then again lengthways. Season with salt and pepper. Cut the cold polenta into slices about 1cm (½ in) across.

Brush a griddle with oil and place over a medium heat to become hot. Lay the slices of polenta on the griddle in 2 portions, and cook for about 3 minutes each side. Keep hot. Grill the asparagus in 2 portions for about 3 minutes each side. Arrange the asparagus and polenta on plates and serve with a mixed salad.

Serves 2:
2 red onions
250ml (9fl oz) vegetable stock
sea salt
80g (3oz) polenta wholegrain maize meal
1 tbsp chopped flat leaf parsley
1 pinch of nutmeg
400g (14oz) green asparagus
white pepper
2 tsp olive oil

PER PORTION:
235 kcal
8 g protein
5 g fat
39 g carbohydrate
1 mg cholesterol

Couscous

an Arabian speciality

with mango

Bring the vegetable stock to the boil, add salt, and stir in the couscous.

Cover and cook on a low heat for about 5 minutes, then draw off the heat,

and leave to swell for about 15 minutes. Meanwhile,

Serves 2:

160ml (5 $^1/_2$ fl oz) vegetable
stock

sea salt

160g (5 $^1/_2$ oz) couscous

2 red onions

3 sticks of celery

1 mango

1 tsp sunflower oil

1 tsp freshly grated ginger

1 tsp cumin

black pepper

$^1/_2$ tsp butter

1 tsp pink peppercorns

peel and chop the onions. Wash the celery and slice

diagonally into pieces 5mm ($^1/_4$ in) thick. Peel the

mango, detach the fruit flesh from the stone, and cut

into roughly 1cm ($^1/_2$ in) dice.

Heat the oil in a frying pan over a medium heat. Fry

the onion and celery for about 2 minutes until

translucent, stirring. Stir in the ginger and cumin.

Add the diced mango and cook gently for another 2

minutes, stirring. Season with salt and pepper.

Fluff up the couscous with a fork, mixing the butter

into it in flakes. Pile on to plates. Garnish with the

mango and vegetable mixture and the peppercorns. Green peas and

yoghurt flavoured with mint make suitable accompaniments.

PER PORTION: 377 kcal • 12 g protein • 4 g fat • 73 g carbohydrate • 3 mg cholesterol

Green cabbage
with herb and Parmesan gratin
with buckwheat

Preheat the oven to 180°C (350°F). Remove the stalk from the cabbage, wash, cut in half, and chop. Wash and peel the potatoes, and cut into dice about 1.5cm (³/₄in) across. Peel and chop the onions.

Heat 1 teaspoon of the oil in a saucepan over a medium heat, and lightly fry the onions and diced potato for about 1 minute, stirring. Pour on the stock. Stir in the cabbage and bring to the boil. Then add salt and pepper, cover, and simmer for about 10 minutes.

Mix the breadcrumbs, Parmesan, parsley, and basil. Transfer the cooked vegetables to an ovenproof dish, and scatter over the breadcrumb mixture. Bake in the middle of the oven for about 10 minutes.

Wash the buckwheat in hot water and drain in a colander. Heat the remaining oil in a frying pan and add the buckwheat. Cook for about 1 minute, stirring. Season with salt, pepper, and caraway. Scatter over the gratin and serve.

Serves 2:

400g (14oz) green cabbage

200g (7oz) potatoes

2 red onions

1 ¹/₂ tsp olive oil

150ml (5fl oz) vegetable stock

sea salt, pepper

4 tbsp wholewheat breadcrumbs

20g (³/₄oz) freshly grated Parmesan

2 tbsp each of chopped parsley and basil

40g (1 ¹/₂oz) buckwheat

1 tsp caraway seeds

power

PER PORTION: 312 kcal • 17 g protein • 7 g fat • 43 g carbohydrate • 6 mg cholesterol

Light cream of

topped with sun-dried tomatoes

carrot soup

Wash and peel the carrots, and slice coarsely. Dice 50g (scant 2oz) of the slices finely, and set aside. Wash and trim the leek, cutting it open lengthways to clean it thoroughly. Take the white part only and slice roughly into rings.

Heat the oil in a saucepan over a medium heat and fry the coarsely sliced vegetables for about 3 minutes, stirring, until translucent. Pour on the stock and bring to the boil. Add the bay leaves, ginger, and marjoram. Cover and cook over a low heat for about 10 minutes.

Meanwhile, cut the tomatoes into very fine strips. Remove the bay leaves from the soup, stir in the buttermilk, and puree the soup with a hand blender until creamy. Season with salt and pepper. Garnish with finely diced carrot, strips of tomato, and chervil.

Serves 2:
250g (9oz) carrots
100g (3 $^1/_2$oz) leek
1 tsp olive oil
400ml (14fl oz) vegetable stock
2 small bay leaves
$^1/_2$ tsp freshly grated ginger
1 $^1/_2$ tsp marjoram
6 sun-dried tomatoes
150ml (5fl oz) buttermilk
sea salt
black pepper
2 tsp chopped chervil

Using buttermilk in soups

Buttermilk makes an ideal substitute for cream when preparing rich soups for a low-cholesterol diet. 100g (3 $^1/_2$oz) of buttermilk contain just 0.5g fat as against 48g for double cream and 19g for single, and only 2mg of cholesterol where double cream contains 130mg and single cream 55mg.

PER PORTION:

14 kcal

5 g protein

4 g fat

21 g carbohydrate

3 mg cholesterol

Miso soup

quick to make and almost fat-free

with vegetables

Serves 2: • 500ml (18fl oz) vegetable stock • 2 tbsp miso • $\frac{1}{2}$ tsp grated ginger • sea salt • pepper

• 3 fresh shiitake mushrooms • 50g (scant 2oz) each of celery, carrots, and leek • 1 tbsp balsamic vinegar

• 2 tbsp chopped chives

Bring the stock to the boil over a medium heat. Stir in the miso, and season with ginger, salt, and pepper. Wipe the mushrooms with a damp cloth, remove the stems, and slice the caps thinly. Wash and trim the vegetables and dice finely. Add the mushrooms and vegetables to the soup. Adjust seasoning to taste with the vinegar. Sprinkle with the chives to serve.

32

PER PORTION: 121 kcal • 4 g protein • 4 g fat • 17 g carbohydrate • 2 mg cholesterol

Lentil soup with

a full-flavoured soup high in fibre

green cabbage

Serves 2: • 100 g (3 $\frac{1}{2}$oz) lentils • 1 onion • 200g (7oz) green cabbage • 50g (scant 2oz) carrots

• 50g (scant 2oz) celery • 1 tsp olive oil • 500ml (18fl oz) vegetable stock • 1 bay leaf • allspice

• 1 sprig of thyme • sea salt • pepper

Place the lentils in 300ml (10fl oz) water. Heat, and boil for 2 minutes. Set aside to stand for 1 hour. Peel the onion. Wash and trim the cabbage, carrots, and celery. Chop all finely. Fry the onion in oil until translucent, pour on the stock and bring to the boil. Add the lentils, vegetables, bay leaf, allspice, thyme, salt, and pepper. Cover and cook for 15 minutes.

PER PORTION: 262 kcal • 16 g protein • 5 g fat • 35 g carbohydrate • 2 mg cholesterol

Bean soup

low-fat, satisfying, and high in fibre

with tofu

Cover the beans with water and boil vigorously for 2 minutes, then draw off the heat and leave to stand for about 1 hour (alternatively, soak overnight in cold water). Then drain. Soak the mushrooms in water for 1 hour. Peel and chop the onion and garlic. Heat the oil in a saucepan over a medium heat, and fry the onion until translucent, stirring. Add the garlic, beans, bay leaves, and thyme, and continue to cook gently for about 3 minutes, turning the food. Pour on the vegetable stock, add the beans, and bring to the boil. Cover and cook for about 45 minutes.

After 30 minutes, cut the mushroom caps into eighths. Remove the stalks. Wash the vegetables. Cut the celery into diamond shapes roughly 1cm (½in) across. Remove the tough stem parts of the tomatoes and dice coarsely. Stir all into the bean soup, and season with salt and pepper. Cover again, and continue cooking for another 10 minutes.

Cut the tofu into roughly 1cm (½in) dice. Stir into the soup, together with the capers. Continue cooking for about another 5 minutes. Remove the sprig of thyme and bay leaves. Sprinkle with the chervil and serve with hot French bread.

Serves 2:

100g (3 ½oz) haricot beans

25g (scant 1oz) dried shiitake mushrooms

1 onion

2 cloves of garlic

2 tsp olive oil

2 bay leaves

1 small sprig of thyme

600ml (20fl oz) vegetable stock

3 sticks of celery

3 bush tomatoes

sea salt, pepper

100g (3 ½oz) tofu

1 tbsp capers

2 tbsp chervil

PER PORTION: 358 kcal • 20 g protein • 10 g fat • 46 g carbohydrate • 2 mg cholesterol

Broccoli curry with

spicy, satisfying, and easy to digest

sweet potatoes

Serves 2:

350g (12oz) broccoli florets
2 miniature corn cobs
2 sweet potatoes (about 200g/7oz)
2 red onions
1 tsp sunflower oil
1 tsp mild curry powder
1 tsp tamari (Japanese soy sauce)
300ml (10fl oz) vegetable stock
sea salt, pepper
1 tsp pink peppercorns
2 sprigs of chervil

Wash the broccoli, corn cobs, and sweet potatoes. Cut the corn cobs diagonally in half. Peel the sweet potatoes and cut into roughly 5cm (2in) dice. Peel, halve, and slice the onion into half rings.

Heat the oil in a saucepan over a medium heat. Brown the onions and sweet potatoes, stirring. Mix in the corn cobs, curry powder, and tamari. Cook together for about 1 minute. Pour on the stock, season with salt and pepper, and bring to the boil. Cover and cook for about 8 minutes on a low heat. Add the broccoli and cook for another 4 minutes.

Serve the curry in bowls, garnished with pink peppercorns and a sprig of chervil. Serve hot flat (naan) bread and rice to accompany.

Curry – popular and versatile

With their invigorating taste, curries are well loved. The spices in curry contain several ingredients that can lower blood cholesterol. Here is a recipe for curry spice mixture: 1/4 tsp each of fenugreek*, cumin*, chili powder*, grated ginger*, fresh mint, and coriander (cilantro) leaves, 1/2 tsp turmeric*, and 1 curry leaf (kari phulia) or bay leaf. Health-promoting spices are marked with an asterisk*

PER PORTION:

310 kcal

10 g protein

5 g fat

57 g carbohydrate

1 mg cholesterol

Artichoke curry

stylish, hot, and low in cholesterol

with tofu

Serves 2:

4 globe artichokes

juice of 1 lemon

1 green pepper

80g (3oz) tofu

2 red onions

1 tsp olive oil

1 ¹/₂ tsp hot (Madras) curry powder

200ml (7fl oz) vegetable stock

sea salt

black pepper

Remove the stems of the artichokes with a single tug. Cut off the leaves and scoop out the "choke" with a spoon. Place the artichoke hearts in the lemon juice, with enough water to cover. Cut open the green pepper and remove the stem, ribs, and seeds. Wash and cut into pieces about 1cm (¹/₂ in) across. Cut the tofu into 1cm (¹/₂ in) cubes. Peel the onions, cut in half downward, and slice thinly across.

Heat the oil in a saucepan over a medium heat. Cut the artichoke hearts into eighths. Fry these with the onion and green pepper for about 3 minutes until translucent, turning constantly. Mix in the curry powder and fry for 1 more minute, stirring. Pour on the vegetable stock and season with salt and pepper. Bring to the boil and simmer for about 3 minutes. Stir in the tofu shortly before serving, return to the boil, and adjust the seasoning.

Serve hot in dishes. Accompany with boiled rice (grains still separate) and yoghurt flavoured with mint.

PER PORTION: 150 kcal • 10 g protein • 5 g fat • 14 g carbohydrate • 1 mg cholesterol

Bean curry
rich in soya and fibre
with tandoori

Wash and trim the beans. Cut in half. Peel the onions and slice thinly into strips. Cut the tofu into 1cm (½ in) cubes. Heat a wok or large, deep frying pan. Add and heat the oil. Fry the onions until translucent, stirring. Add the beans. Fry, stirring constantly, for about 5 minutes. Add and stir in the tandoori spices, curry powder, and thyme. Pour on the vegetable stock and bring to the boil. Season with salt and pepper. Cook in the open pan on a low heat for about 3 minutes. Season generously to taste.

Serve the bean curry hot, in bowls. Heat flat (naan) bread in a frying pan to accompany.

Serves 2:

600g (1 ¼ lb) green beans

2 red onions

80g (3oz) tofu

1 tsp olive oil

1 tsp tandoori spice mixture

1 tsp mild curry powder

1 tsp thyme

200ml (7fl oz) vegetable stock

sea salt

black pepper

Tofu

Soya beans and soya products like tofu have a beneficial effect on cholesterol levels. Soya can lower blood cholesterol, especially the harmful LDL type. The beans in this recipe, the onions, and the low-fat method of preparation are further plus points.

PER PORTION:

150 kcal

10 g protein

5 g fat

17 g carbohydrate

1 mg cholesterol

power

Sicilian

with capers and green olives

caponatina

Cut the red pepper in half and remove the stem, ribs, and seeds. Wash the tomatoes and aubergines, remove the stem area, and cut into pieces about 2cm ($^3/_4$ in) across. Peel the onion and garlic and chop finely. Pit the olives, cut in quarters lengthways, and set aside.

Heat the oil in a saucepan over a medium heat. Fry the onions, garlic, and red pepper for about 1 minute until translucent, stirring. Add the aubergine and cook together gently for about 2 minutes. Then stir in the tomatoes. Season with salt and pepper. Cover and cook over a low heat for about 5 minutes. Stir in the olives and capers. Season with honey and vinegar for a sweet-and-sour taste. Serve hot or warm with flat (naan) bread or potatoes boiled in their skins.

Serves 2:

1 red pepper

3 ripe tomatoes

1 aubergine (eggplant) (about 250g/9oz)

1 large red onion

1 clove of garlic

8 green olives

$^1/_2$ tsp olive oil

sea salt

pepper

2 tbsp (large) capers

1 tsp honey

2 tsp balsamic vinegar

power

PER PORTION: 95 kcal • 4 g protein • 4 g fat • 13 g carbohydrate • 0 mg cholesterol

Braised vegetables
a taste of Greece – delicious hot or cold
in earthenware

Serves 2: • 1 onion • 1 small chilli • 100g (3 ¹/₂oz) each of green beans, courgettes (zucchini), and aubergines (eggplant) • 5 tomatoes • salt • pepper • 2 tbsp each of chopped parsley and basil
• 1 tsp olive oil

Soak an earthenware cooking pot in water for 10 minutes. Peel and chop the onion. Wash and trim the chilli, beans, courgettes, aubergines, and tomatoes. Cut into pieces and season with salt and pepper. Mix in the herbs. Transfer the vegetables to the earthenware pot. Add 6 tablespoons of water and the oil. Replace the lid and put into a cold oven (middle). Set the oven at 200°C (400°F) and braise for 1 hour.

PER PORTION: 80 kcal • 5 g protein • 2 g fat • 11 g carbohydrate • 0 mg cholesterol

Chinese
with tongku mushrooms and soy sauce
potato stew

Serves 2: • 12 Chinese (tongku) mushrooms (Chinese supermarket) • 6 potatoes • 2 carrots
• 200g (7oz) green beans • 1 clove of garlic • 1 tsp sunflower oil • 1 tsp grated ginger • salt • pepper
• 2 tbsp soy sauce • 2 tbsp chopped parsley

Soak the mushrooms in water for 10 minutes. Peel the potatoes and carrots. Wash and trim the beans. Cut the mushroom caps and the vegetables into pieces. Peel and chop the garlic. Heat the oil and fry the ginger, garlic, vegetables, and mushroom caps. Pour on 125ml (4fl oz) water. Season with salt and pepper. Cover and cook for 5 minutes. Sprinkle with parsley to serve.

PER PORTION: 156 kcal • 7 g protein • 2 g fat • 27 g carbohydrate • 0 mg cholesterol

Chickpea
a fibre-rich dish for chilly days
stew

Cover the chickpeas with water in a saucepan, and boil vigorously for 2 minutes.

Remove from the heat, cover, and leave to stand in the water for about 1 hour

(alternatively, soak overnight in cold water). Peel and chop the

garlic finely.

Heat the oil in a saucepan over a medium heat and fry the

garlic briefly until translucent. Stir in the chickpeas. Pour on the

vegetable stock and bring to the boil. Cover and simmer for

about 15 minutes.

Meanwhile, wash the parsnip and carrots. Peel and grate them

coarsely. Cut the leek open lengthways and wash it thoroughly.

Take just the white part, and cut into thin strips. Mix the

vegetables with the chickpeas. Stir in the saffron. Bring to the

boil, cover, and cook for about 3 minutes on a low heat.

Wash the tomatoes and courgettes. Remove the tough stem

parts and dice finely. Add to the stew. Season with salt and

pepper. Sprinkle with chopped coriander leaves to serve. Potatoes baked or boiled in

their skins make a good accompaniment.

Serves 2:
80g (3oz) chickpeas
1 clove of garlic
1 1/2 tsp olive oil
500ml (18fl oz) vegetable stock
100g (3 1/2 oz) parsnip
2 small carrots
100g (3 1/2 oz) leek
1 1/4 tsp powdered saffron
2 tomatoes
100g (3 1/2 oz) courgettes
(zucchini)
sea salt
pepper
1 tsp coriander (cilantro) leaves

power

PER PORTION: 237 kcal • 12 g protein • 6 g fat • 31 g carbohydrate • 2 mg cholesterol

Grilled oyster
sweet and sour – with white cabbage and apricots
mushrooms

Serves 2:
2 shallots
400g (14oz) white cabbage
50g (scant 2oz) dried apricots
2 tsp olive oil
¼ tsp caraway seeds
sea salt
pepper
400g (14oz) oyster mushrooms
2 tsp herbs of Provence
2 apples (Cox's Orange)
1 tbsp cider vinegar
1 tbsp sunflower seeds
1 ½ tsp mustard seed
2 tbsp chopped chives

Peel and chop the shallots. Wash the cabbage, cut away the stalk, and cut into diamond-shaped pieces. Cut the apricots into small strips. Heat 1 teaspoon of oil in a lidded frying pan or a wok, over a medium heat. Fry the shallots briefly until translucent, stirring. Add the cabbage, and fry lightly for 5 minutes, tossing the contents of the pan. Stir in the apricots, caraway, salt, and pepper. Cover and cook over a low heat for 3 minutes.

Wash and trim the mushrooms, and season with salt, pepper, and herbs of Provence. Heat a griddle, and brush it with the remaining oil. Grill the mushrooms on the griddle for about 2 minutes on each side. Remove and keep hot. Wash the apples in hot water, core, and dice (with skin if liked). Season the cabbage with cider vinegar and stir in the apples. Cover and cook for 3 minutes until al dente. Toast the sunflower seeds in a dry frying pan over a medium heat, stirring. Grind the mustard seed coarsely in a pepper mill. Arrange the cabbage and mushrooms on plates and serve sprinkled with the sunflower seeds, mustard seed, and chives.

power

PER PORTION: 304 kcal • 13 g protein • 8 g fat • 43 g carbohydrate • 0 mg cholesterol

Steamed salmon on

with fresh redcurrants

a bed of red cabbage

Serves 2:

400g (14oz) potatoes

1 ¹/₂ tsp olive oil

sea salt, pepper

250ml (9fl oz) vegetable stock

2 bay leaves

¹/₂ piece lemon grass

2 fillets of salmon 80g/3oz each)

1 shallot

300g (10oz) red cabbage

1¹/₂ tbsp cider vinegar

1 tsp honey

1 pinch of caraway seeds

80g (3oz) redcurrants

Preheat the oven to 170°C (340°F). Wash and slice the potatoes (in their skins if liked). Stir in 1 teaspoon of oil, adding salt and pepper. Spread on a baking sheet and cook in the middle of the oven for 15 minutes, turning once.

Bring 200ml (7fl oz) stock to the boil with the bay leaves and lemon grass. Steam the salmon over this in an expandable steamer for about 20 minutes.

Peel and chop the shallot. Wash the red cabbage, cut away the stalk, and slice finely into strips. Heat a wok or large frying pan over a medium heat. Add and heat the remaining oil. Fry the shallot until translucent. Add and lightly fry the red cabbage for 3 minutes. Then add the remaining stock, the cider vinegar, honey, caraway seeds, salt, and pepper. Simmer gently for 5 minutes. Wash the redcurrants, strip them from the stems, and stir into the cabbage. Arrange on plates, set the salmon on top, and serve with the potatoes.

Salmon

Although salmon is an oily fish, it has a good P/S quotient of 1.4 (see pages 4-5), giving it a healthy plus. It is rich in omega-3 fatty acid, which can lower cholesterol levels.

PER PORTION:

340 kcal

19 g protein

13 g fat

36 g carbohydrate

29 mg cholesterol

power

Cod with vegetables

marine fish makes a very low-cholesterol dish

Wash and peel the kohlrabi, and cut into large matchsticks. Wash and peel the beetroot, halve, and slice. Bring 100ml (3 ¹/₂ fl oz) of the stock to the boil and cook the kohlrabi for 2 minute. Remove. Cook the beetroot in the same stock for 5 minutes.

Add the lemon juice to the remaining stock and boil. Add the cod, cover, and simmer slowly for about 8 minutes without boiling. Remove the fish and keep hot. Reduce the cooking liquid by a third. Season with salt, pepper, horseradish, and sour cream.

Peel and chop the shallots. Heat the oil and fry the shallots until translucent. Add the kohlrabi and beetroot, and toss over a low heat for 3 minutes. Stir in the poppyseed. Transfer to plates and place the cod on top. Add the carob bean flour to the sauce and puree with a hand blender. Pour over the fish. Serve with gnocchi.

Serves 2:
100g (3 ¹/₂ oz) kohlrabi
150g (5oz) beetroot
200ml (7fl oz) vegetable stock
juice of ¹/₂ lemon
2 cod steaks (80-100g /3-3 ¹/₂ oz each)
sea salt, pepper
1 tsp grated horseradish
1 tbsp sour cream
2 shallots
1 tsp sunflower oil
¹/₂ tsp ground poppyseed
1 pinch of unroasted carob bean flour

Cod

Cuts of cod are an ideal basis for many low-cholesterol dishes. Cod contains only a trace of fat, and has the lowest cholesterol content of the various fish types, 30mg per 100g of fish.

PER PORTION:

141 kcal

19 g protein

3 g fat

8 g carbohydrate

32 mg cholesterol

power

Pike-perch

with saffron and thyme

with fennel

Wash and trim the fennel and cut into fine strips. Peel the onions, cut in half, and cut into fine half-rings. Wash the orange in hot water, dry, and grate a quarter of the zest. Squeeze out the juice and set aside.

Heat 1 teaspoon of the oil in a frying pan over a medium heat. Lightly fry the onions and fennel over a low heat for 5 minutes, stirring. Add the saffron, salt, pepper, lemon thyme, orange zest, and orange juice. Mix in. Cook for 5 minutes uncovered, stirring occasionally.

Meanwhile, brush the fish with the remaining oil and season with salt and pepper. Wash and trim the spring onion. Chop or cut into fine strips, including the green part. Heat a griddle over a medium heat, and grill the fish for about 4 minutes on each side on a low heat. Arrange the fish on top of the vegetables. Scatter the spring onion on top to serve. Suitable accompaniments are millet, rice, or grilled potatoes.

Serves 2:

2 fennel bulbs

2 medium-sized onions

1 unwaxed orange

2 tsp olive oil

a few strands of saffron

sea salt

pepper

$\frac{1}{2}$ tsp lemon thyme

2 pike-perch fillets (80-100g/ 3-3 $\frac{1}{2}$ oz each, middle cut)

1 spring onion

Cooking pike-perch the low-fat way

Pike-perch (zander) is a delicate, lean fish. 100g (3 $\frac{1}{2}$ oz) of pike-perch have a fat content of just 0.7g. A low-fat method of cooking is important to the cholesterol-conscious. The fish has a fine texture and excellent flavour. No figures are yet available for the cholesterol content.

PER PORTION:

200 kcal

26 g protein

4 g fat

14 g carbohydrate

0 mg cholesterol

Purslane
with fresh grapes
with chicken

Preheat the oven to 100°C (210°F). Peel and chop the shallots. De-stem the purslane, wash, and drain it. Remove any fat from the chicken breasts. Season with salt and pepper. Brush a frying pan with a little oil and place it over a medium heat. When hot, fry the chicken breasts for 4 minutes on each side, occasionally easing them away from the bottom of the pan. Transfer to the oven to keep hot. Heat $1/2$ teaspoon of oil in the hot frying pan and fry the shallots until translucent. Stir in the purslane. Season with nutmeg, lemon juice, salt, and pepper. Cover and cook gently for 5 minutes. Wash the grapes and remove from the stems. Wash and trim the spring onion, and chop the white and green parts, separating them and reserving the green. Wash and chop the celery. Heat the remaining oil and fry the grapes, the white part of the spring onion, and the celery for 4 minutes.

Wash the buckwheat in hot water and drain. Toast it in a dry frying pan until the fragrance begins to rise. Add it to the grapes. Season with salt and pepper. Arrange the purslane, grapes, and chicken breasts on plates, and sprinkle with the green spring onion.

Serves 2:
2 shallots
200g (7oz) purslane
2 skinless chicken breasts
(80-100g/3-3 $1/2$ oz each)
sea salt
pepper
1 $1/2$ tsp grapeseed oil
1 pinch of nutmeg
juice of $1/2$ lemon
100g (3 $1/2$ oz) grapes
1 spring onion
3 sticks of celery
100g (3 $1/2$ oz) buckwheat

PER PORTION: 431 kcal • 33 g protein • 7 g fat • 59 g carbohydrate • 60 mg cholesterol

Quail en
wrapped to bake gently
papillote

Peel and chop the onion. Cut the red pepper in half and remove the stem, ribs, and seeds. Cut into diamond-shaped pieces. Season the quail with salt and pepper.

Heat ¹/₂ teaspoon of oil in a frying pan and brown the quail until golden. Remove. Put the remaining oil in the hot pan. Fry the onions and red pepper for 2 minutes until translucent. Remove from the heat.

Preheat the oven to 180°C (350°F). Peel and chop the garlic. Wash the tomatoes, remove the stem parts and cut into six segments. Wash the courgettes, remove the stem parts, cut in half lengthways and slice. Wash and trim the mushrooms, and cut in half. Add the vegetables and garlic to the red pepper and onion. Season with salt and pepper.

Place two sheets of parchment on top of each other for each papillote. Place some vegetables and a quail on each, with a bay leaf, a sage leaf, and ¹/₂ sprig of rosemary. Wrap the parchment around the contents and fold to seal. Transfer to a greased baking sheet. Place in the oven and cook for about 15 minutes.

Serves 2:

1 red onion

1 red pepper

2 quail (about 100g /3 ¹/₂ oz each)

sea salt, pepper

1 tsp olive oil

1 clove of garlic

3 small vine tomatoes

150g (5 oz) courgettes (zucchini)

100g (3 ¹/₂ oz) small button mushrooms

2 bay leaves

2 sage leaves

1 sprig of rosemary

4 sheets of baking parchment

* Quail – an elegant, low-fat option

A special and different choice for the cholesterol-conscious: quail are low in fat and cholesterol by comparison with other poultry. They have a fat content of just 2.3g and a cholesterol content of 45mg per 100g of meat.

PER PORTION:

121 kcal

16 g protein

2 g fat

0 g carbohydrate

30 mg cholesterol

Scorzonera

with crisp strips of turkey and pears

vegetable melange

Peel and halve the onion, and slice into half-rings. Wash and trim the Brussels sprouts and slice. Wearing gloves, peel the scorzonera. Slice.

Serves 2:
1 small red onion
200g (7oz) Brussels sprouts
200g (7oz) scorzonera
1 tsp sunflower oil
sea salt
pepper
1 pinch of caraway seeds
150g (5oz) skinless turkey breast
1 pear (Williams)
1 tsp walnut oil

Heat ¹/₂ teaspoon of oil. Lightly fry the onions and scorzonera over a low heat for 3 minutes. Add the sprouts. Season with salt, pepper, and caraway seeds. Cover and cook gently for another 5 minutes.

Cut the turkey breast into strips. Season with pepper. Heat the remaining oil over a medium heat. Fry the turkey strips for 5 minutes until golden. Season with salt and keep hot.

Wash the pear in hot water. Peel if wished, core, and dice. Mix with the scorzonera. Stir in the walnut oil. Continue cooking the vegetables for another 3 minutes. Correct seasoning. Arrange on a plate with the turkey strips. Serve with baked potatoes, seasoned with rosemary.

Turkey breast is versatile

Skinless turkey has an important role in low-cholesterol cuisine, because 100g contains only 1g of fat and 60mg of cholesterol. Finely sliced and lightly fried, it goes well with almost all vegetable and salad dishes.

PER PORTION:

182 kcal

23 g protein

4 g fat

12 g carbohydrate

45 mg cholesterol

Sweet kasha

A fibre-rich delight for health-conscious food lovers

with citrus salad

Heat a frying pan over a medium heat. Reduce the heat to low and toast the buckwheat in the dry pan, stirring, for about 4 minutes until the fragrance begins to rise.

Wash the orange in hot water and grate 1 teaspoon of zest. Grind the poppyseed in a coffee grinder, or pound it using a mortar and pestle. Bring the milk, orange zest, poppyseed, salt, cardamom, and cinnamon to the boil in a saucepan. Stir in the buckwheat and return to the boil. Cover and leave on a low heat for about 20 minutes to absorb the liquid.

To make the citrus salad, trim the peel with the white pith and skin from the orange, grapefruit, and mandarin. Cut the fruit in half horizontally and cut out the fruit flesh in bite-sized pieces. Catch and reserve the juice. Wash the mint, pat dry, and shred finely. Mix the mint, fruit juice, vanilla, and 2 tablespoons of the honey.

Serves 2:

60g (2oz) buckwheat
1 unwaxed orange
1 tbsp poppyseed
150ml (5fl oz) low-fat milk
sea salt
2 cardamom pods
1 pinch of ground cinnamon
1 pink grapefruit
1 mandarin
1 tbsp fresh mint leaves
few drops of vanilla extract
3 tbsp honey
1 tsp chopped, unsalted pistachio nuts

Shortly before serving, stir the remaining honey into the creamy buckwheat kasha. Arrange on plates, decorate with the citrus salad, and pour over the fruit sauce. Sprinkle with the pistachio nuts.

PER PORTION: 286 kcal • 7 g protein • 4 g fat • 55 g carbohydrate • 4 mg cholesterol

Kefir with

refreshing and fat free

raspberries

Serves 2: • 200 g (7oz) raspberries • $\frac{1}{2}$ bunch basil • 1 tbsp granulated raw cane sugar

• 300ml (10fl oz) kefir (or probiotic yoghurt drink) • 3 tbsp maple syrup • generous few drops of

vanilla extract

Sort the raspberries. Wash the basil, shake dry, remove the leaves from the stem, and shred

enough to fill 2 tablespoons. Mix the raspberries, basil, and sugar. Set aside. Mix the kefir, maple

syrup, and vanilla. Pile the raspberries on to plates, pour on the kefir mixture, and decorate with

basil leaves to serve.

PER PORTION: 210 kcal • 6 g protein • 3 g fat • 35 g carbohydrate • 8 mg cholesterol

Quinces with

provides beneficial pectins

cinnamon yoghurt

Serves 2: • 2 quinces • 100ml (3 $\frac{1}{2}$ fl oz) orange juice • 4 tbsp honey • 1 star anise • 1 $\frac{1}{2}$ sticks of

cinnamon • 1 tsp grated lemon zest • 1 pinch of unroasted carob bean flour • 30g (1 oz) yoghurt

• 1 $\frac{1}{2}$ tsp ground cinnamon

Peel, core, and dice the quinces. Bring the orange juice to the boil with 2 tablespoons of the

honey, the star anise, cinnamon sticks, and lemon zest. Poach the quinces in the juice for 5

minutes until al dente. Lift out the quinces and remove the spices. Bind the fruit sauce with

carob bean flour, pour over the quinces, and transfer to a cold place. Mix the remaining honey

with the yoghurt and ground cinnamon, and serve with the fruit.

PER PORTION: 201 kcal • 6 g protein • 3 g fat • 36 g carbohydrate • 8 mg cholesterol

Vanilla pears with

light as a dream

quark cream quenelles

Place the quark in a bowl with the yoghurt, purée, and honey. Beat together until creamy. Cover and place in the refrigerator.

Meanwhile, wash and dry the pears. Core them and cut each into 8 slices. Bring the pear juice to the boil with the lemon juice, vanilla, and maple syrup. Poach the pear slices in the juice for about 3 minutes over a low heat, covered. Lift out with a slotted spoon and set aside to cool. Bind the syrup with the carob bean flour, stirring. Set aside to cool.

Arrange the pear slices on plates. Shape the quark cream into neat ovals (quenelles) between two spoons, and arrange beside the pear. Surround with the syrup and garnish with mint leaves.

Serves 2:

100g (3 $^1/_2$oz) low-fat quark

3 tbsp low-fat yoghurt

6 tbsp unsweetened purée of sea buckthorn (or jujube or raspberry or cloudberry)

2 tbsp honey

2 Williams pears

100ml (3 $^1/_2$fl oz) pear juice

juice of 1 lemon

few drops vanilla extract

2 tbsp maple syrup

2 pinches of unroasted carob bean flour

2 mint leaves

Carob bean flour

Carob bean flour is fat free and cholesterol free. This special unroasted flour is neutral in flavour, and makes a versatile binding agent. It comes from the seeds of the carob fruit. The outer pods are used to make carob, the cocoa substitute.

PER PORTION:

250 kcal

9 g protein

2 g fat

49 g carbohydrate

0 mg cholesterol

power

Mixed berry

full of refreshing fruit and low in calories

dessert with rice

Serves 2:

300g (10oz) mixed berries, fresh or frozen

100g (3 ¹/₂oz) morello cherries (use bottled fruit)

few drops of vanilla extract

2 tbsp honey to taste

2 pinches of unroasted carob bean flour

50g (scant 2oz) round-grained rice (Arborio)

170ml (6fl oz) low-fat milk

1 tsp grated lemon zest

sea salt

3 tbsp maple syrup

1 ¹/₂ tsp ground cinnamon

Preheat the oven to 150°C (300°F). If using fresh berries, wash, sort, and allow to drain. Thaw frozen berries slowly. Drain and reserve the juice from the cherries. Bring 100ml (3 ¹/₂oz) cherry juice to the boil with a few drops of vanilla. Sweeten with honey to taste. Add the berries and cherries, return to the boil, and simmer for 2 minutes over a low heat. Stir in the carob bean flour to bind. Set aside to cool.

Place the rice in a lidded pan or casserole with the milk, a few drops of vanilla, the lemon zest, and salt. Bring to the boil, cover, and simmer for about 10 minutes. Transfer to an ovenproof dish if necessary and cook in the middle of the oven for 30-40 minutes according to packet instructions. Stir in maple syrup and cinnamon and transfer to a ring mould. Turn out on to the plates and spoon the fruit mixture into the middle.

Prepare in advance

Both the fruit dessert and the rice in this recipe contain plenty of fibre, and can be enjoyed hot or cold. They can be prepared hours in advance; even the day before. The fruit dessert is fat free and delicious on its own, without the rice, as an ultra-light option.

PER PORTION:

295 kcal

5 g protein

2 g fat

63 g carbohydrate

2 mg cholesterol

Bulghur wheat
high in vitamins, low in calories
with melon

Boil about 150ml (5fl oz) water and stir in the bulghur wheat, vanilla, cardamom, and 1 teaspoon of lemon zest. Cover and simmer for about 5 minutes. Set aside and leave to stand.

Serves 2:
60g (2oz) bulghur wheat
generous few drops of vanilla extract
1 ¹/₂ tsp cardamom
zest of 1 unwaxed lemon
150g (5oz) redcurrants
1 lime
1 tbsp honey
1 ¹/₂ tsp grated ginger
2 tbsp raw cane sugar
¹/₂ small, sweet melon (Cavaillon)
8 mint leaves

Wash the redcurrants, drain, and strip from their stalks into a bowl. Remove the peel and pith from the lime. Dice the fruit, catching the juice. Stir the honey and ginger into the lime juice and mix with the redcurrants. Carefully add the lime fruit.

Loosen the bulghur wheat with a fork and stir in the raw cane sugar. Spoon on to plates. Peel and halve the melon and remove the seeds. Cut into six slices and arrange in a fan shape beside the bulghur wheat. Serve with the redcurrants and mint leaves.

Ginger and cardamom
Both spices help to lower blood cholesterol and blood fat levels. They also promote digestion. Ginger stimulates the metabolism and the circulation. Best flavour is obtained when it is fresh, and used sparingly. It can be grated, diced, or sliced according to the particular recipe.

PER PORTION:

228 kcal

6 g protein

1 g fat

51 g carbohydrate

0 mg cholesterol

power

Gooseberry and

with a sharp but tempting sweetness

almond snow

Preheat the oven to 170°C (340°F). Wash, trim, and drain the gooseberries.

Heat a lidded pan over a medium heat. Add 2 tablespoons of honey, the

vanilla, and the gooseberries to the pan, cover, and

cook for about 6 minutes over a low heat. Transfer to

a gratin dish.

Beat the egg whites until stiff. Whisk in the

remaining honey. Carefully fold in the ground

almonds and 1 teaspoon of lemon zest.

Pile the almond snow on top of the gooseberries.

Level and smooth the surface. Brown in the middle of

the oven for 10 minutes.

Wash the strawberries and mint. Trim and halve the strawberries. Serve

the crisp gooseberry snow on plates with the strawberries and decorated

with mint.

Serves 2:

300g (10oz) gooseberries

3 tbsp honey

generous few drops of vanilla extract

2 egg whites

6 tsp ground almonds

zest of 1 unwaxed lemon

6 strawberries

6 mint leaves

What to do with the egg yolk

Egg white is cholesterol free. Not so the yolk, which
is high in fat and cholesterol. Surplus egg yolks can
be frozen. They then keep for about 8 months. Use it
to make lemon curd. Note: always freeze egg yolks
and whites separately.

PER PORTION:

193 kcal

7 g protein

6 g fat

27 g carbohydrate

0 mg cholesterol

power

Index

Low cholesterol – low fat

Abbreviations

tsp = teaspoon
tbsp = tablespoon
kcal = kilocalories

Nutritional analyses in each recipe refer to the metric measurements.

Most of the ingredients required for the recipes in this book are available from supermarkets, delicatessens and health food stores. For more information, contact the following importers of organic produce:-
The Organic Food Company, Unit 2, Blacknest Industrial Estate, Blacknest Road, Alton GU34 4PX; (T) 01420 520530 (F) 01420 23985
Windmill Organics, 66 Meadow Close, London SW20 9JD
(T) 0208 395 9749 (F) 0208 286 4732

Fermented wheat juice is produced in Germany by Kanne Brottrunk GMBH
(T) 00 49 2592 97400 (F) 00 49 2592 61370

Further information on German food importers is available from The Central Marketing Organisation (T) 0208 944 0484
(F) 0208 944 0441

First published in the UK by
Gaia Books Ltd, 20 High Street,
Stroud, GL5 1AZ

Registered at 66 Charlotte St,
London W1P 1LR
Originally published under the title
Low Cholesterol, Low Fat

© Gräfe und Unzer Verlag GmbH
Munich. English translation copyright
© 1999 Gaia Books Ltd
Translated by Elaine Richards in association
with First Edition Translations Ltd,
Cambridge, UK.

Nutrition advisor: Angela Dowden

Reproduction: MRM Graphics Ltd,
Winslow, UK.
Printed in Singapore by Imago

ISBN 1 85675 166 X

A catalogue record for this book is available in
the British Library

10 9 8 7 6 5 4 3 2 1

Caution

The techniques and recipes in this book
are to be used at the reader's sole
discretion and risk.
Always consult a doctor if you are in doubt
about a medical condition.

Elisabeth Dopp worked for some time as a
reader for large publishing houses. She has been
a writer of cookery books since 1985 and a
health educator in nutrition for the Association
for Independent Health Counselling. She also
delivers courses in nutrition and cookery.

Christian Willrich comes from Alsace. He has
been a chef in French gourmet restaurants since
1980, and an author of cookery books since
1988.

Jorn Rebbe trained as a cook in a Japanese
hotel. He has been contributing to cookery
books since 1995. He has been a dietetically
qualified cook since 1997.

Photographs: FoodPhotography Eising, Munich

Susie M. and **Pete Eising** have studios in
Munich and Kennebunkport, Maine/USA.
They studied at the Munich Academy of
Photography, where they established their
own studio for food photography in 1991.

Food styling:
Monika Schuster

Feng Shui Cooking
Recipes for harmony and health
Fahrnow, Fahrnow and Sator
£4.99
ISBN 1 85675 146 5
More energy and wellbeing from recipes that balance your food.

Beauty Food
The natural way to looking good
Dagmar von Cramm
£4.99
ISBN 1 85675 141 4
Natural beauty for skin and hair - eating routines for a fabulous complexion.

Vitamin Diet
Lose weight naturally with fresh fruit and vegetables
Angelika Ilies
£4.99
ISBN 1 85675 145 7
All the benefits of eating fresh fruit and vegetables plus a natural way to weight loss.

Low Cholesterol - Low Fat
The easy way to reduce cholesterol, stay slim and enjoy your food
Döpp, Willrich and Rebbe
£4.99
ISBN 1 85675 166 X
Stay fit, slim and healthy with easy-to-prepare gourmet feasts.

Energy Drinks
Power-packed juices, mixed, shaken or stirred
Friedrich Bohlmann
£4.99
ISBN 1 85675 140 6
Fresh juices packed full of goodness for vitality and health.

Anti Stress
Recipes for acid-alkaline balance
Dagmar von Cramm
£4.99
ISBN 1 85675 155 4
A balanced diet to reduce stress levels, maximise immunity and help you keep fit.

Detox
Foods to cleanse and purify from within
Angelika Ilies
£4.99
ISBN 1 85675 150 3
Detoxify your body as part of your daily routine by eating nutritional foods that have cleansing properties.

Mood Food
Recipes to cheer you up, revitalize and comfort you
Marlisa Szwillus
£4.99
ISBN 1 85675 161 9
The best soul comforters, the quickest revitalizers and the most satisfying stress busters.

To order the books featured on this page call 01453 752985, fax 01453 752987 with your credit/debit card details, or send a cheque made payable to Gaia Books to Gaia Books Ltd., 20 High Street, Stroud, Glos., GL5 1AZ. e-mail: gaiapub@dircon.co.uk or visit our website www.gaiabooks.co.uk